TOMORROW'S CHILDREN

Also by Tsolagiu M.A. RuizRazo:

Spirit of the White Wolf Woman

Tomorrow's Children

A CHEROKEE ELDER'S GUIDE TO PARENTING

Tsolagiu M.A. RuizRazo

World Edition, USA
New Tazewell, Tennessee

Published by:
World Edition, USA
PO Box 1284
New Tazewell, TN 37824

Editor: Ellen Kleiner
Book design and typography: Angela Werneke
Cover design: Angela Werneke
Cover illustration: David Coyote Benedict
Author photo: Felicia R. Chardon

Printed in the United States of America on acid-free recycled paper

Publisher's Cataloging-in-Publication Data

RuizRazo, Tsolagiu M. A.
    Tomorrow's children : a Cherokee elder's guide to parenting /
    Tsolagiu M. A. RuizRazo
        p. cm.
        LCCN 2003094157
        ISBN 0-9715227-0-7

    1. Child rearing. 2. Parenting. 3. Cherokee philosophy. I. Title
HQ769.R769 2003   649'.I
                              QB103-200621

10 9 8 7 6 5 4 3 2 1

This book is dedicated to

my granddaughter, Anineyata

my daughter, Tanawaki

and the parents of every future caretaker

of Mother Earth

In Gratitude . . .

First and foremost, I give thanks to the Creator and all the forces of nature.

To my husband, Rahkweeskeh, thank you for your understanding.

To my daughter Felicia, of World Edition, USA, thank you for participating and standing by me.

To Maria de Alvear, of World Edition, Germany, thank you for your support.

To Ellen Kleiner, of Blessingway, thank you for your guidance, patience, and open-mindedness.

And to Angela Werneke, thank you for giving this book such an incredible look.

Contents

Part III: Children As Future Caretakers of Mother Earth

Preface

Raising children is a joyful part of natural life, but to nurture them well we must first be in balance, understand our goals, and have a deep sense of personal freedom. As a Cherokee teacher, mother, and grandmother, I am aware that Cherokee culture offers considerable wisdom for parents in today's society. The purpose of this book is to share such wisdom, along with many traditions, so it may contribute to better child-rearing and, by extension, greater nurturing of the earth.

Part One of the book focuses on preparing for parenthood in the Cherokee way—by balancing the self, assessing personal circumstances and their suitability for child rearing, and setting goals for family life. Balance allows us to better learn from our surroundings and behaviors. Once we achieve balance, we can look forward to healthier relationships with others and more nurturing interactions with Mother Earth. Ultimately, these achievements make us more effective parents.

Part Two illuminates aspects of pregnancy, birth, and child rearing from the viewpoint of Cherokee culture, including special considerations for pregnancy, birthing methods and ceremonies, and traditional ways of raising children. Bringing children into the world entails numerous responsibilities to the family and society. It also calls for vigilant attention to the environment, for according to Cherokee tradition children are the future caretakers of Mother Earth.

To accentuate this aspect of nurturing children, Part Three expands on today's great need to nurture Mother Earth. Traditional Cherokee wisdom tells us that parents are themselves children and guardians of the earth. As such, they are perfectly suited to teach tomorrow's children how to honor and protect our planet—roles of exceptional importance for the future of humanity.

"An Inventory for Balanced Parenting," appearing at the end of the book, provides a reliable tool for evaluating your strengths and weaknesses in order to restore balance. It is best used before conception as well as throughout the child-rearing journey.

Concluding each portion of the book is a meditation to assist in personal healing. Relaxing the body and quieting the mind allows you to get in touch with and transform feelings such as anger and pain, receive messages from the Spirit World, or simply achieve peace after a busy day. By keeping a parenting journal on the information received during these meditations, you will be able to track your accomplishments.

For me, there is nothing more essential than the health and happiness of all people of all races and religions, especially children. Throughout my life I have guided and taught children in various settings. For many years, I offered classes in theater makeup, helping troubled students become enthusiastic performers. In elementary schools I painted clown faces for school-organized parades, while in high schools I taught courses in skin care, hair care, and makeup for young girls.

In later life, I focused more on assisting people in better developing their minds, bodies, and spirits, using my abilities to see and communicate with the Spirit World. In connection with this work, I established the Traditional Native Survival and Cultural Center, Inc., a nonprofit agency benefiting North American Indians and indigenous people of Mexico and South America. I also founded TMAR Human Development and Stress Release, Inc., an organization focused on teaching methods for pain relief and connecting with nature.

I first became aware of my special gifts at age seven, when I was at school attending Mass and heard voices and sounds of thunder, felt strangely faint, and later woke up on the floor. Following this event I had other experiences with the Spirit World, soon discovering that I was capable of seeing and communicating clearly with spirits, including people who had died years before. Gradually, my ability to see and communicate with spirits strengthened, enabling me to heal individuals at great distances.

Today I am a deep medium with many abilities. I can travel to the sky world, as well as unknown dimensions, and I have been blessed with the gift to serve people who are experiencing strange and dangerous psychic phenomena in their homes. My Cherokee name, Tsolagiu, means the woman who walks in the Spirit World, and it is by working hard to maintain traditional ways that I keep my spirit strong. Cherokee culture teaches that Mother Earth helps alleviate sadness and pain. We are taught to care for Mother Earth in return, by not abusing her or robbing her of trees, plants, or minerals, for their qualities make her strong. To further sustain our relationship with the natural world, we give morning or evening prayers of thanks to earth and sky and continually develop various aspects of ourselves.

Because the Creator gave me the gift of communicating with the Spirit World, I have been able to help countless people and find healing exceedingly rewarding. How fulfilling it is to see a formerly crippled person walk, to witness a woman giving birth after being told she couldn't have children, to watch an endangered baby breathing without oxygen support. While participating in a healing of any sort, I remain aware not only of personal satisfaction but of working for the good of humanity.

As a woman of Cherokee heritage, I embody a circular education. A member of the Wolf Clan of the Cherokee people, I was raised by my great-aunt in the Ozark Mountains of Missouri, where I established a strong sense of identity. I spent my childhood happily in harmony with nature, surrounded by trees, animals, and water. There I was encouraged to explore my abilities to see, hear, and speak with spirits, while finding my weaknesses and strengths through meditation. During my years of formal schooling, I learned the lifeways of white society. Then as an adult I rediscovered the ways of my indigenous ancestors, renewing contact with my inner self and greatly strengthening it. Again I began going into the woods to listen to the teachings of the wind, trees, animals, and water spirits. With this closing of the circle, the wealth of knowledge I was gleaning from the Spirit World took its place beside the teachings of some remarkable people.

I am now a grandmother. As I teach my daughter how to raise her daughter with connections to the Creator and to Mother Earth, I am struck by the urgent need for such bonds in today's world. This book, rich with traditional Cherokee ways, is meant to keep the river of wisdom flowing.

PART I

Preparing for Parenthood

Attaining
Inner Freedom

*N*otice how trees on a mountaintop move slightly as the wind ripples through their branches, and how the sun makes the shadows of trees dance on the earth. As we pay attention to our surroundings, they teach us about the beauty of another life—a life of freedom.

It is important to gain *inner* freedom in order to be good parents. One way to do this is by going inside ourselves, looking around inch by inch, and facing then releasing any negative emotions we encounter. The first sensation we may come upon is fear—the dread of uncovering feelings that might cause us discomfort. But with patience and determination we can push aside this fear and begin facing the negative emotions of pain, anger, sadness, or loneliness. We get rid of each one by taking slow deep breaths all the way into the abdomen, holding the breath while concentrating on the negative feeling, and letting the breath out with force. This should be done five times or until the feeling has been released.

Another way to inner freedom involves releasing the pain carried from childhood that contributes to who we are now. To find this freedom, go to the mountaintop and give your pain to the Creator. As you release it, the wind will carry away the pain and you will be healed. Work to attain this freedom, for then you can be true to yourself and better face what life has to offer.

An additional means to inner freedom involves reducing the stresses of daily life. For effective stress reduction, breathe deeply from your abdomen, with your jaws fully apart, and let out a spontaneous sound. While working with all these exercises, it is helpful to remember that if our spirits were not strong, we would not be here searching for freedom.

The search for inner freedom is sometimes hard for society to accept; yet it is essential for learning about your particular spirit and connecting with it in day-to-day life. If you choose to independently cleanse yourself of hurts and other painful emotions, notice that the release of each one draws you closer to your spirit. It helps to meditate for fifteen to twenty minutes: as you begin to sense a calmness inside, ask the Creator to help you let go of whatever blinds you to your true nature. In doing this each day, you come to know yourself as a powerful resource capable of distinguishing right from wrong.

If instead you decide to work toward inner freedom in a spiritual group, make sure you are learning true teachings about the spirit and making a genuine connection with it rather than with the emotions. This will prevent you from giving your power away.

Because pregnancy is such a significant step in life, it is best approached in a state of inner freedom. Women who are unburdened of negativity and worries learn to pay closer attention to their bodies, better understand how they function, and adapt more easily to the many changes pregnancy brings. They come to know *inwardly* the most healthful foods for their bodies and the importance of drinking plenty of water, exercising in conducive ways such as walking or swimming, and practicing stillness several times a day. When you relax, your unborn child learns how to be calm.

Cherokee culture explicitly encourages the attainment

of inner freedom before pregnancy. When a man and woman decide they are ready to have a family, the woman is traditionally given time to think about child rearing and its many responsibilities. She spends a day or more alone with herself and the Creator, at liberty to explore her inner world. Then she speaks with an elder, a respected person of knowledge. The elder may ask her if she has had dreams or visions of a child, or of anything related to children. If she has, the elder will interpret their meaning for her. If she hasn't, the elder will furnish answers to her questions.

Whether or not you are inclined to seek the counsel of an elder, consider finding inner freedom before deciding to have a child. That way you will be less likely to confuse hormonal changes that stimulate yearnings for a baby with deeper desires rooted in love for children and dedication to future society. Freedom creates the space for choosing wisely and for avoiding unwanted pregnancy. To help young girls over age ten avoid unwanted pregnancy, parents are advised to be aware of the girls' contact with boys and, if necessary, engage the girls in other kinds of activities. Older women, more accomplished in the ways of freedom, are encouraged to look within and decide if being a parent would genuinely fit their lifestyle.

Achieving inner freedom gives us the perspective, strength, and wisdom to someday soar like an eagle. Imagine riding on the back of an eagle, with a gentle rain falling on your face, the wind in your hair, or the sun warming your back. Feel the bird's soft feathers and the heat of its body as you glide through the clouds and up over a brilliantly colored rainbow. Mountains are in front of you now and you hold on tight, preparing to weave among the peaks with utmost precision. Your energy is high. Excitement floods your entire body, filling you with joy. You are weightless, thoughtless, painless, worry free. You want to become a part of this eagle and soar forever, seeing far and wide, resilient enough to ride any current, and keenly attuned to the ways of nature's landscape.

The Place
of Freedom

*T*here is a place of freedom—a place where all of nature's creatures go to find freedom. We can follow the wind to this place and be free in a natural way. Or we can get there by aligning our spirit with any other aspect of nature, or with the Creator. Elders, too, can help for they have experienced the many ripples of life. When we reach this place of freedom, nature knows and responds in perceptible ways.

To help people find the place of freedom, I take them into the mountains or the woods and have them work on resolving problems while observing the responses of the natural world. When they are still too focused on personal problems, flies and other insects will bother them. But once they have cleared themselves by meditating, nature will no longer annoy them. Although it requires patience, finding the place of freedom is illuminating because it allows us to become increasingly in tune with nature.

Some years ago, a lady came to me with a strong fear of being in the woods, which she overcame using this method. One day after going into the woods, she said, "I'm so excited. The bugs and flies didn't bother me!" From then on, whenever she visited the woods birds perched nearby and animals approached without frightening her. Even snakes slithered by without upsetting her, for she had learned to speak to them in a quiet voice. This place of peace and harmony is the place of freedom.

Another time, a large, burly man came to work on his anger toward his wife and children, who had insisted he deal with it. At first he had no idea why he was angry, but over time he began to link the rage to incidents in his past. Still, he had no clue how to release it. I asked him to go to a stream and be with the water. Like a petulant child, he skulked off mumbling, "I don't know if I'm going to like this." As it turned out, he didn't like it at all—the water swirled about unpredictably and often drenched him from head to toe. His next day's assignment was to set up camp beside the stream and cook his meals there, meditating and journaling throughout the day. He did as he was told and returned the next morning complaining about how the water had kept him awake for hours on end. After releasing his aggravations, he went back to the campsite, where he remained for three days.

During his next appointment he explained that the water was much calmer and he'd had a vision in which he learned he was ungrateful and must stop chastising the people he loved. I remarked on how much more relaxed he seemed, at which point this stocky man broke down and cried, asking the Creator for forgiveness and saying he wanted to be a better person. Over the next several years he broke free of the rage, found the way to his spirit, and became kind and loving toward his wife and children.

In the place of freedom nature mirrors back the fears or negative emotions that are imprisoning us at the time. As we work to clear ourselves of them, nature begins conspiring with us, releasing each chain of bondage by increasing our awareness of our innermost state of being. This is a place of great transformative power.

Teachings of
the Wind Spirit

*L*et the wind blow across your face and through your hair. Let the wind caress your body. This embodiment of spirit is all around. Listen to what it says.

There is much to be learned by listening to the wind. Go out on a blustery day and hear what the wind people have to say. Then invite them to carry away whatever negativity you are holding and to clear the cobwebs from your mind. When the wind has calmed, notice how much freer and stronger you feel.

The teachings of the wind are powerful, as everyone around me was to learn one clear summer day. My husband and I were in a building about to do a doctoring ceremony on several women with health problems when I noticed among them a particularly debilitated woman and asked her to wait about an hour so I could work separately with her. After my husband and I had completed our work with the others, I felt the need for a break before this woman's doctoring ceremony, so I went into the nearby woods. There I asked the wind spirit to cleanse the land and the building so the woman's healing would be strong.

About twenty minutes later a deafening roar came from the direction of the building. It was the wind, howling like an old freight train, shaking the earth, and causing the trees' branches to bend nearly to the ground. A moment later it headed straight toward me. I held up my hands and said, "I am here," whereupon it let out a swishing roar and suddenly became very still about two feet in front of me. I returned to the building and completed the last ceremony, fortified by the wind's teachings of strength and healing medicines.

It's not every day that spirit barrels in like a freight train. But always it is in the air. Apprentice yourself to the wind and you will know the way forward.

Healing
Pain

*A*ccording to Cherokee teachings, there will always be pain in life. If there were no pain, we would never know joy. If everything were perfect, there would be no need to strive for goals.

Yet, although pain has meaning, it need not remain so strong as to make us ill, which it can easily do. One way to heal pain is by working with the Creator. Begin by sitting in a place of comfort and safety, either indoors with soft lights or outdoors in nature. Then find the bones inside you that hold agony from distressing experiences, and bring the light of the Creator into your body and to your aching bones. Visualize the Creator taking this pain, putting it in a place where it will hurt no one else, and bonding it there. Next, ask the Creator to show you how to avoid pain-producing experiences in the future.

Finally, listen very quietly for the Creator's guidance. If at first you hear no messages, continue to listen from time to time until they register. When you feel stronger, go into nature and seek further guidance from the trees, animals, and birds.

This practice can relieve physical pain ranging from a headache to the throbbing of a stubbed toe, as well as many types of emotional pain. Although it cannot eliminate all pain in life, it can at least help you achieve more balance and harmony.

Emerging
from Darkness

*E*ach of us is part of the Creator, who understands every language, including the language of darkness. During our lifetime, we all pass through places of darkness, tested by the Creator to see if we will do good things in times to come. While in these places, we might cry out from the pain of life, worry about loved ones, or feel anxious about making ends meet. Darkness can be caused by any circumstance—such as loss, illness, sleep deprivation, drugs, or alcohol—breeding thoughts or behavior patterns that obstruct our awareness of the Creator. To endure these hard times, whatever their cause might be, look deep inside yourself and try to see the light beyond the darkness.

Emerging from darkness takes hard work. One

approach is to tape-record your negative experiences and, replaying the tape, give a positive interpretation to each one. Another is to keep a journal of the difficulties you are going through and reread the entries from a more positive point of view.

If you choose to do this work on your own, be truthful with yourself. When first coming out of the darkness, you will be tested to see if you are strong enough to stay in the light. Being truthful at such times means acknowledging thoughts and behaviors that are disrespectful of others or dishonoring of the Creator. Have you been putting people down, or talking rudely to them? Have you been lying or cheating? As soon as you become aware of a dark thought or behavior, catch it in action and correct it. For instance, if you are about to insult someone, stop and say nothing; if you have already spoken harsh words, rectify the pain you may have caused.

In replacing negative thoughts and actions with positive ones, we move toward respect of all creation. Drawn closer to all that is natural, we return to the light, for we have proved our strength by overcoming the isolation caused by our negativity. At that point, we regain our self-respect.

Once you have returned to the light, do your best to keep it within your range of vision. The more you stay where the Creator is, the more likely you will be of good mind, good heart, and good spirit.

Creating a
Positive Outlook

*H*ow do you start your day? Do you wake up with an attitude? Do you dwell on disheartening tasks, such as paying bills or going to a job you don't like? Are you weighed down by thinking the life you lead keeps you from fulfilling your needs? Or do you look on the positive side of events?

A positive outlook first thing in the morning can keep you strong the whole day through. If you are prone to a negative outlook, consider ways to make it more affirmative. First, tell yourself that you want to change. Then think about the factors that contribute to your negative outlook. Finally, begin altering them to create more enjoyable circumstances. As you do, ask the Creator for help in broadening your outlook, making your life fuller, and better fulfilling your needs.

For a more rewarding day, wear brighter colors to cheer yourself up. Say good morning to family members and co-workers. Greet people by their name and when you see them, smile. Go to lunch with a friend, and while you are there laugh, talk, or just listen receptively. Walk erect, with your head up and shoulders back. Offer a kind word to a stranger, or graciously open the door for someone.

Along with starting the day in a lighter way, you can gain a more positive attitude through ongoing expressions of gratitude. Every morning, give thanks to the night you have lived through so you could greet the new day. At night, give thanks to the day you have just experienced. Day and night, give thanks for all that the Creator has given you, including the hard times, for these too add to your growth and learning.

Finding
Inner Peace

Where is the peace we are all seeking? It is inside us, but we have to work to find it. To get to this place of serenity, we need freedom and contact with self. While free of tension, inwardly quiet, and accepting of our destiny, we discover the peace for which we are searching.

Meditation, if practiced consistently, is a sure path to inner peace. To follow this path, start by meditating for fifteen minutes three days a week, then progress to half an hour or a full hour.

A good way to find inner peace after a long, busy day is to soak in a hot bath for forty minutes to an hour. Begin by running the bathwater with a little sage or juniper oil. When the tub is full, set a few white or yellow lit candles around the bathroom, dim the lights, burn incense, then slip into the water. To help unwind from the day's pressures, breathe in deeply through your nose and exhale through an open mouth. As you release the buildup of stress, a calmness inside will allow you to sort out any confusion you may be carrying. Soon you might feel as if you are beginning to float.

Discovering inner peace through relaxing activities is important for connecting with the Spirit World. Often, while walking through the woods, I feel as if I am floating because everything within me is calm, letting me relate to the surrounding world. I can hear the sounds of the winged ones around me, smell the aromas of the earth, and feel the wind's embrace.

Gaining
Spiritual Identity

Who we are is a mystery with clues hidden in the natural world. We are part of all that comes from the Creator—the earth, the sky, the mountains, the water, the animals, the beautiful flowers that grow in forests, the wind, the clouds, Grandmother Moon, and the darkness that slips over her during an eclipse. Even our bodies come from the Creator, reflecting the balance between male and female energies in all of life. Our destiny is to become aware of our spiritual identity so we can live the life given to us by the Creator.

Cherokee culture focuses on gaining spiritual identity through contact with the Spirit World, which we achieve by connecting with the elements of nature. To establish such connections, we take time to speak to the many aspects of Mother Earth—trees, plants, rocks, four-leggeds, rivers, the wind, and the sky world with its clouds, moon, and stars. Every aspect of the natural world has a spirit capable of teaching us about the life force that defines who we are and how we function in the world.

Physical contact with nature is extremely informative. Hugging a tree for five minutes gives you direct evidence of Mother Earth's warmth. If you pay close attention to this energy, you will have a clearer sense of the life force that flows within you.

Like tree spirits, the stone people are very much alive. Mountains are large and strong stone people; smaller stone people live in riverbeds, fields, the woods, and elsewhere on the earth. A memorable encounter I had with stone people occurred while walking in the mountains and suddenly hearing voices, then a drumming sound. Heading in their direction, I came to the edge of a river, where I could make out distinct words.

"I am here," said a voice from the riverbank.

On the earth, just inches from my feet, I found a stone person talking. So I said hello, studied his face, and asked if he was speaking to me.

The stone person immediately replied, "Yes."

"What do you want?" I asked.

"I want you to take me," he said.

Having learned not to take stone people home without a reason, I asked, "Why do you want to go home with me?"

"To help you," he answered.

No sooner did I pick him up than I heard a voice from the stone person that had been beside him, saying, "Take me too."

Honored by his request and noticing his distinct face, I asked, "Well now, who are you and why must I take you?"

"Because I work with him," the second stone person said, matter-of-factly.

I picked him up and asked them both what I was to do with them. They told me their duty was to heal people and that they work together. To this day, the two stone beings remain with me and they have healed many people.

In addition to establishing contact with the forces of nature to learn how the Creator works with you and through you, consider the guidance of a teacher. Question several teachers about things that interest you, and see if their answers ring true to you. Then select a teacher who emanates a strength you can feel. Since there are many false teachers in the world, continue searching until you find a true teacher who is right for you.

When you have come to know your spiritual identity, you will be able to open your heart to all that is around you without losing your way. Such awareness will also help you distinguish life forces from negative feelings, which you will then be able to recognize and clear. The greatest gift received in gaining spiritual identity is an unwavering sense of being close to the Creator—so close that in any moment you can be guided to walk in balance with all the forces of nature.

Meditation

- Sit or lie in a comfortable place indoors or out, and breathe deeply. While inhaling, push your stomach outward like a big balloon; then let the air out slowly, allowing your stomach to return to normal. Do this 8 times, or until you are totally relaxed.

- Visualize yourself as a strong, good person parenting a child, and see what feelings this evokes.

- Breathe deeply again for about 15 minutes, taking in all the good feelings of strength while relaxing your body.

- When you are ready to end the meditation, come out slowly to the count of 10 and open your eyes.

- Remain in place for a while, then get up and, in your parenting journal, record what you have received.

PART II

Pregnancy, Birth, and Child Rearing

Ceremonial Approaches to Pregnancy

Cherokee tradition includes forms of preparation for pregnancy that call upon the wisdom of the Spirit World and the support of clan members. First, the couple makes an appointment with an elder who counsels people wanting to start a family. During their session, the elder asks them about their feelings toward each other, their home and work situations, their prospects for child care, and whether the grandparents-to-be will assist in raising the child. This session is meant to help the couple think more deeply about their plans and determine if they are individually mature enough to handle the responsibilities of having a child. Such visits continue until the elder decides the couple is ready for the next step.

The couple then schedules an appointment with a

medicine person. The proper way to approach a medicine person is with a gift of means, such as money or an object of great personal value, along with a gift of sacred tobacco. After presenting their gifts, the couple is cleansed with plant medicines. The woman then explains that she is ready to bring a child into the world and wants to know more about her health. The medicine person looks into the Spirit World for this information and reports it to the couple. If an illness is seen, the appropriate healing ceremony is performed, which may require an additional visit. Otherwise, the couple arranges for the final ceremony.

The last ceremony before pregnancy is usually performed under the stars. First, the medicine person cleanses the couple to remove negativity and darkness from them, and then purifies the surroundings. Next, the medicine person asks the Spirit World to send to the mother's womb a spirit with strength, a good heart, and willingness to carry the Creator's gifts. The Creator is then told that the mother will protect and watch over this child throughout its life. After the closing of the ceremony, the couple turn their attention to the conception of their child.

The Gifts
of Pregnancy

Because the Cherokee people believe that the Creator chooses a spirit's parents, once conception has taken place the child's spirit is considered a gift from the Creator. The womb, the "land of the Creator," is regarded as a place of safety, love, and nurturing. Parents, envisioning the hugging offered by the womb, sing or speak softly to their unborn child.

When it is time for this sacred gift to be born, the mother tells her little one that a passage is about to begin. She might say something like this: *Hold my hand, for I am about to take you on a journey. Here in the land of the Creator, where your spirit life began, warmth enveloped you. The fluid around you was pure, and the food nourishing to your growing body. Despite swift energy currents of the rivers, mountains, and valleys in your midst, you felt secure in this*

place of laughter and singing, of love and caring. Hold my
hand tightly, for the time has come to leave the womb and
enter the outer world.

Conception brings not only the gift of a child's spirit
but also unique opportunities to face other mysteries of life.
Your spirit might remind you of how *you* were before birth—
insights that can help you correct imbalances in your day-to-
day existence. Also, as you attune to the child in your womb,
you might recognize his inherent inner freedom and simple
love for life, and resolve to reinforce these qualities through
a connection with nature as he grows older.

Traditional Cherokee culture offers the additional gift
of family participation. Everyone gets involved in preparing
for the birth of a child, including the extended family and
other clan members. The father-to-be helps by remaining
close to the expectant mother, making life easier for her by
taking care of domestic needs such as hunting for food,
gathering firewood, cleaning the home, and keeping it pro-
tected against harsh weather. As necessary, other relatives
assist by cooking, cleaning, and attending to the expectant
mother. Grandparents, especially, take pride in caring for her,
as well as assisting with domestic chores. Clans, which have
come through the mother's line since the beginning, have a

vital function at this time: they support the prospective parents by taking the expectant mother to doctor's appointments or by transporting their other children to school.

These gifts of pregnancy make the time of childbearing less burdensome and isolating than it otherwise might be. Moreover, they imbue it with an atmosphere of cooperation and celebration.

Parenting Decisions

*P*regnancy is a time filled with parenting decisions. Will you be a single parent or will both parents be in your child's life? Do you want the father to help with the birth? If the father would like to be there, consider his feelings. Also ask yourself how you would feel with him guiding you through your breathing and the pain of delivery. If the idea makes you uncomfortable, it may instead be best to find a parent, relative, or friend to attend the birth.

Consider, too, whether you feel at ease with your doctor or midwife, and other chosen care providers. Do they help you feel comfortable about the birth process? Are you able to ask questions and have them answered in a way that you can understand? Choose practitioners who will give you clear explanations of your birthing options and the potential consequences of any pain or procedures. With good communication, you can feel confident letting them assist you through any discomforts that arise.

Other parenting decisions to address during pregnancy involve caring for your child after birth. Do you and your partner agree on how the child will be raised? How will you teach the baby her culture? Do you want her to grow up in the mainstream urban society or a more rural setting? What religion will she be exposed to? Parents who during pregnancy have no prejudice concerning color, race, or religion, and who agree on the focus of cultural teachings, avoid later disputes about raising their child.

Some of the most crucial decisions to make during pregnancy relate to the expectant mother's lifestyle. In this regard, it is beneficial for parents of any culture to follow traditional Cherokee teachings, which are the following. Rather than risk exposure to anything that might traumatize herself or the unborn baby, the expectant mother focuses on taking care of herself and her home, filling her days with happiness. She refrains from participating in ceremonies, because the medicines used in them are considered too strong during this time of purification. For the same reason, she knows to avoid alcohol, drugs, cigarettes, and sleep deprivation. Similarly, her partner does his best to make this time pleasant for her. As the pregnancy progresses, usually beginning around the fifth month, the mother begins to talk, sing, and read to her unborn child, paying attention to the child's responses so she comes to know her preferences.

The expectant mother also maintains respect for the wisdom of elders, drawing support and knowledge from their words. She later passes this knowledge on to her child so it may guide future generations. In Native American culture, elders still play a significant role in child rearing, and their wisdom is passed down to each new generation. This is done not only to strengthen family ties but to assure continuity of the Cherokee way of life.

A Time
of Beauty

$\mathcal{A}$ child's journey to this world is a time of beauty for the prospective parents. They have talked about bringing a life into the world, and now that it has been conceived they look forward to the birth with great anticipation. They may even sense the spirit of the child serving as a "tour guide," informing them of the direction his life is to take. To do their part well, they seek out a caring birth practitioner who will attend to the expectant mother, monitor the baby's growth, and explain the stages of pregnancy and birth. They know that the more they understand, the easier and more advantageous the pregnancy will be.

As the time of beauty continues, the expectant mother becomes keenly aware of the life inside her body. She feels its growth and marvels at the many changes taking place inside her. Inwardly, she begins caring for this new life through gentle communication and love.

Outwardly, however, each stage of the passage calls for special considerations. For the first three to four months of pregnancy, you may have "morning sickness," or nausea, in either the morning or the evening. In addition to getting advice from your doctor or midwife, you could try the following traditional Cherokee remedies:

⧈ Keep crackers by your bed, and eat a few before beginning the day.

⧈ Don't drink water first thing in the morning.

⧈ Eat light, small meals throughout the day.

Sometimes nothing alleviates morning sickness, but eventually it will stop. You might also experience mood swings, dizziness, fainting, cramps, and crying for no reason, but these symptoms, too, will disappear as time passes.

By the fourth month of pregnancy, your body may start changing radically. This is usually the time for looser clothing and for being able to hear the baby's heartbeat. During the fourth month you can find out the sex of the baby if you wish. While some people prefer to wait until the birth, others like to have this information in advance so they can shop for the new arrival and friends can more easily plan baby showers.

Over the last months of pregnancy, every day can seem endless as you look forward to your new arrival with increased anticipation. Around the eighth month you may want to joyfully prepare the baby's room, decorating it in the most welcoming manner possible. The ninth month is best reserved for resting and giving thought to the birth setting, where this time of beauty will give way to the thrill of welcoming your emerging child.

Cherokee
Birthing Traditions

The Cherokee people make special preparations for child-birth. Long ago, when Cherokee women birthed their babies outdoors in nature, they would choose a place in advance for this sacred passage and ask specially trained women to assist in the delivery. Today, birth takes place indoors after the woman has decided whether she wants to have her child in a birthing center, in the hospital, or at home. The father may wish to be present at the birth to help her, an offer she is generally encouraged to accept with an open mind.

If the birth is to take place out of the home, the prospective parents visit the site together. There they are informed about how best to prepare for the birth. They learn about sound nutrition and are given vitamins. In addition, they are taught exercises to help prepare for labor, as well as breathing and other techniques to use during the birth.

If the mother-to-be has chosen to have her child at home with a midwife in attendance, the midwife explains the events of birth in advance so the couple will know what to do during labor. Typically she also ensures that a doctor is on hand in case of complications. She lets the couple know that once contractions have begun, she will coach the mother, telling her when to push and when to breathe. The father or another person the mother selects can help her with the breathing. At the mother's request, grandparents and other family members may also be present.

Whatever site is chosen for the birth, the event is ushered in with ceremony. As birthing time approaches for an expectant mother planning to deliver away from home, someone she has chosen comes to perform a ceremony, sending greetings to the Creator while burning incense or herbs to connect to the Spirit World, welcoming the life about to arrive, and inspiring the mother during the delivery. For a birth at home, elders may be asked to come sing special songs and burn particular medicines. This may be followed by a gathering of all family members, invited to celebrate the new birth with traditional dances, songs, and drumming. The birth of a child is an occasion to be enjoyed by many good spirits.

While giving birth, the mother will experience both joy and pain, but the pain is a pain of joy and will quickly fade. Once the child has announced herself to the world, she is first given to the mother, then taken by the midwife to be cleaned and tucked into a warm blanket while others in attendance congratulate the parents. After the mother has rested, the midwife helps her breastfeed the baby. Usually, by the time the new arrival is nestled in her arms and free to learn about the outer world, the mother's pain has gone, leaving both parents with feelings of pure joy.

After Childbirth

According to Cherokee tradition, it is the mother who takes care of the new baby. Once the mother and child are home, or as soon as the midwife has left, the grandparents and other family members remain nearby to make sure mother and baby are not separated. Grandparents today do not always live with the new family, as they did in the past. Even so, they continue to play an active role in family life, helping to raise their grandchildren and teaching the parents the ways of the nation.

After the birth, the baby is kept home for at least one month to protect him from excessive stimulation in his open and vulnerable state. For the first week after the birth no one but the immediate family comes to the home, and the only people to handle the child, other than the parents, are the grandparents and siblings. The baby is kept wrapped in a blanket with hands at his sides, leaving him free to look about without touching anything around him. Later, when taken outside, he is wrapped in the same way, laced to a cradle board, and carried on his mother's back. After about two months the baby is carried unwrapped in the mother's arms, although she still does not let the public touch or kiss him.

Beginning about two weeks after the birth, other family members come to see the baby, often bearing gifts. During these visits, siblings assist the mother and newborn, later taking care of him when the mother is busy. Only after a month or so does the family invite friends to come see the baby.

Also about this time, an elder is called to perform a naming ceremony for the child. The elder will either receive the child's name in a dream or go into the Spirit World to receive the name from the child's maternal ancestors, into whose clan the child was born. After the name is found, the child is cleansed with herbs and given his name during the ceremony, which is held at the home and attended by family and friends, all of whom bring food for the celebration meal.

The child's name, which reflects his spirit, describes his characteristics, how he will live life, and the duties he will perform, or it may simply portray a beautiful aspect he possesses. Family members, after being given its full meaning, are expected to call the child by this Cherokee name, which stays with him for life. When the child eventually learns to speak to the Creator, he will use his Native name to announce himself, thereby letting the Creator know of his place in the Spirit World. At all other times, the child's Native name tells him who he is and how he must conduct himself.

The weeks after childbirth are extremely formative. During this time, it is important to honor your baby's unique gifts and to shield him from too many worldly influences. That way he will retain an inner sense of his spiritual origins. The more aware of them he is, the easier it will be for his spirit to continue its development as he finds his way in the world.

The Growing Child

Showing love for your baby and nurturing her spirit through early contact with nature encourage her emotional and spiritual development. Hold her close and breastfeed if possible, to establish a strong bond between you. For feedings, find a special place to sit with her, such as a rocking chair or other comfortable chair. If you have toddlers, you could sit with them on a couch and explain that you are feeding the baby. Also hold your baby close while rocking her, singing to her, or playing gently with her. Rocking, singing, and humming will help your baby fall asleep, as well as allow her to feel at ease sleeping in bed with you, if you desire. Also let your baby adjust to household sounds, since if the home is kept too quiet she may have a hard time getting to sleep in the presence of movement or noise.

During her second month of life, take your baby out into nature, and begin to foster within her a strong connection with the natural world. Cherokee wisdom tells us that nature is our teacher, suggesting that babies in touch with many aspects of nature are learning a great deal. And as they grow, these teachings grow. When I take walks with my two-year-old granddaughter and she sees something in the natural world that interests her, we talk about it then I identify it by name, which she repeats, further deepening her relationship with it. To encourage similar traits in your baby, insist on respect for all of nature and avoid instilling within her a fear of anything natural. She can then grow up respectful and unafraid of natural forces.

As the months pass, continue showing love for your child and nurturing her spirit. When she cries out with the pain of teething, hurt fingers, or skinned knees, offer comfort. If you are preoccupied at such times, it might be tempting to say, brusquely, "I am busy" or "Wait till later." But while we do need to free ourselves before we can free our children, we must also focus on their concerns. To unburden yourself quickly, remember that you were once a child feeling the same kind of pain go away as your parents comforted you. Infants and toddlers who receive immediate love, care, and hope grow up giving love, care, and hope. They not only reflect these energies back to us but also extend them into their aspirations in life.

It is just as important to demonstrably love your child and nurture her spirit beyond the years of toddlerhood. This you can do by sustaining her contact with nature and gradually introducing cultural lifeways associated with the Spirit World. In Cherokee culture, children are given Native clothing and toys. They are served Native foods such as corn prepared in various ways, fry bread, squash, and other mainstays of the Indian diet, developing a taste for them early on. They also wear traditional regalia at gatherings and ceremonies.

When consistently nurtured both emotionally and spiritually, children maintain their sensitivity to these subtle yet powerful energies. All the while, they grow in balance, gaining strength, resilience, and an increased sense of their place in the world. As they grow in balance, their spirit blossoms.

Learning to
Walk the Edge

or Native children who have grown up in their culture, spending much of their young lives on a reservation, it is difficult to go out into society. The Indian people call this precarious transition "walking the edge." Children walk the edge of their lives best by being strong and practicing survival skills in all circumstances. It is therefore necessary for Native parents to teach their children not only how to live within traditional culture but how to walk the edge with sturdy steps.

If your child will be making this transition, begin preparing him in advance by introducing him to the mainstream culture's survival skills, including how to get work, how to handle money, and how to find room and board. Also help him get accustomed to the ways of society, such as how food is prepared and the meaning of verbal expressions, especially slang, that are unknown to him.

There is no security for children walking the edge. While facing its challenges, they must maintain contact with their inner self in order to gain self-sufficiency. Therefore, concentrate on helping your child get in touch, and stay in touch, with his inner spirit. This is what will keep him from walking the edge for the rest of his life.

Native children who grow up not on a reservation but in a city, town, or small community have already walked the edge. As a result of their repeated interactions with society, they often face difficulties, including problems with alcohol, drugs, or crime. If your child is likely to encounter these types of challenges, start to address them early on in conversation. Reinforce your discussions with steady guidance in maintaining contact with his inner self no matter what might be happening in his world. If he ends up enmeshed in alcohol, drugs, or crime, provide ongoing support in dealing with the problems and in turning his life around so he can find hope for a better future.

Teaching about Inner Spirit

*E*very child is born with an inner spirit to guide them. But before it can reveal its gifts, it needs to be developed through teaching. Indigenous people are encouraged to contact this spirit while young and to nourish it throughout life.

To help your child develop her inner spirit, show her how to recognize this part of herself in her first few years of life. Since connections with the inner spirit come alive only in a state of freedom, let her have as much freedom as possible during this time. Then, when she is five or six, begin teaching her to distinguish between right and wrong, good and bad, explaining the differences to her. Wise choice-making feeds the growth of inner spirit.

Unfortunately freedom in the early years of exploration is often squelched. We hamper a child's freedom by telling her "no" too frequently or by hitting her. To steer your child away from causing harm *without* diminishing her freedom, use alternative ways of controlling unacceptable behavior. Also urge your child to gain inner freedom by releasing negative emotions. If she is angry or frustrated, let her beat a large pillow or work out with a punching bag and gloves, aware that the purpose of such activity is to discharge these emotions. Participation in sports is another means for getting rid of pent-up negativity. The nonharmful release of these emotions opens major pathways to the freedom needed in the quest for inner spirit.

Once you have begun teaching your child how to find her inner spirit, provide her with opportunities to make good choices. If, for example, she has a friend who behaves in hurtful ways, talking about it with her can help her resolve not to join in these activities. As a result of such decisions, her spirit will develop and eventually begin to reveal its special gifts.

In Cherokee culture, as gifts of the spirit come to expression we prepare the child to use them. Parents, grandparents, elders, and clan mothers all watch the child, beginning at an early age. When she comes to them describing an experience that reflects an attribute of the spirit—such as having a vision, talking with another spirit, or showing an ability to heal—they listen intently. Careful not to reinforce the behavior from the outside, they may say, "That is very interesting," and wait for the child to come back later, telling of similar experiences. If she does, then when she is about ten years old, an elder will take her to see someone knowledgeable in her particular gift, who will then guide the parents in helping her develop it and use it to do the work chosen for her.

I was among the children seen to be multigifted. As my spirit developed, I was therefore given many responsibilities. Today, in addition to being a seer, healer, and elder who converses with the Spirit World, I work with other children of Cherokee ancestry so they, too, may develop their gifts. Children who grow up aware of the inner spirit and its gifts become adults capable of living in balance and harmony. Although society may attempt to indoctrinate them into negative lifestyles, telling them how to think or behave, they are able to turn inward and find their true direction in life.

The School Years

*A*fter parental guidance and nurturing in the early years, school is the next layer of foundation for a happy and fulfilling life. When your child first begins school, you might be inclined to shed tears. Go right ahead since it reflects your love for him. For consolation as he heads into the world of new friends and classmates, remember that he has stored everything you have taught him and is now somewhat independent. If you wish, repeat a teaching that can help fortify his inner strength and independence in a world without the comforts of love.

During the school years, you and your child are sure to disagree at times, due to lack of communication or a breach in empathy. Our children forget that once upon a time we also were young and rebelled against our parents, while we forget that we sometimes saw our parents' limit-setting as a sign of caring. So establish healthy rules, and in times of disagreement keep to them. Your consistency will help your child gain insight and responsibility. For example, my mother would often say, "You can't go out with friends till you've finished your chores around the house," and hearing this I would get upset. Ultimately I learned to be responsible for my share of the housework, but not until starting my first job did I understand *why* my mother had taught me such things.

In addition to giving consistent guidance, it is important to listen to school-age children individually, since each one has special needs and desires. A good way to focus on your child's concerns is by arranging evening get-togethers to discuss issues about school, friends, and family. If you listen with a clear mind, your replies will be good teachings.

Although in Cherokee society guidance depends on discipline, its forms have changed over the years. In the past, children were disciplined in front of everyone by the village medicine person. Today, elders counsel children about problem behaviors and monitor the resulting changes. If the elders cannot solve a problem, help is sought among people of our cultural ways outside the nation. Still, as always, discipline is reinforced through household duties. School-age children often take care of younger siblings when parents are busy. Eventually, in addition to caring for siblings, doing school lessons, and learning their native language, they also help with cooking and sewing or do bead work to sell.

Throughout the school years, respect is paramount in Cherokee culture. Children are taught to respect themselves, their family members, their teachers and elders, people who do sacred work for the community, the earth, and all the Creator's life forces. As a result, they gain pride in their gifts of the spirit and in their Native traditions, understanding that although others in the world may have different perspectives, they can maintain their own culture and thus lead more fulfilling lives.

Maintaining the Cherokee culture has become vital in recent times because the survival of our ways has been continually threatened. For instance, over the course of about two hundred years our people were forbidden to speak the Cherokee language—a dialect containing words with potent meanings that have no English equivalent. Soon our children began speaking of things that were barren of meaning in the context of our traditions, such as jail, love, and church. Long ago we had no word for jail; there were no jails. We had no word for love; there was caring for all. Nor did we have a word for church; the Creator was everywhere all the time. Later, as the ban on our language was lifted, we realized that at no point had we lost our knowledge of the Spirit World. Over the last ten to fifteen years, most school-age children of Cherokee ancestry have recognized the value of maintaining Native traditions because, unlike many other children, their people are certain that there is a Spirit World and that it is very powerful.

Youth and
the Teen Years

*T*oday's youth require their parents and elders for guidance. They want to talk to people who understand their problems in a world so full of hurt, anger, and death. They need to be constantly reminded about the good spirit of life and ways in which the forces of Mother Earth can help them.

Between the ages of eleven and thirteen, many youth undergo considerable physical and emotional strain, resulting in upheavals that few are equipped to handle. It can be very frustrating for people of this age not to understand what is happening to their bodies, minds, and emotions, which tend to shift unpredictably. One moment they're happy and laughing, then suddenly they're sad and crying, or angry. They need to know it's okay to have these feelings and that it is possible to deal with situations that arise. Above all, they want to know that you are there to help them through this turbulent time.

In Cherokee culture, such care is reflected in a ceremony celebrating a young woman's transition to adulthood. A young woman announces, sometimes a year in advance, when it is time for the ceremony to take place. As the celebration approaches, older women help prepare her dress and also take her to a special place to pass down their knowledge about womanhood. There they tell her about "Moon Time," the menstrual cycle, and how it prepares her for motherhood, emphasizing that women's bodies are sacred and should not be abused with men. Other people prepare food for the celebration and buy or make gifts for the young woman to give to her helpers, who in turn give gifts to her. As the time of the celebration draws near, a man is chosen to honor her at the ceremony, playing a role similar to an uncle. During the ceremony, various people speak and then the celebrants break out in song and dance.

A young man receives guidance, as well. During his early teen years his parents select an elder to counsel him until he turns seventeen, at which point a ceremony is performed celebrating his entry into manhood. The ceremony usually takes place at the time of the new moon, and preparations for it begin a year before. Over a period of two or three days, older men share their knowledge of how a man is to conduct himself before marrying and how he is to then treat his wife and support his household. Clothing is made; participants for the ceremony are chosen; gifts are assembled; food is prepared; a ceremonial sweat house is built; and singers and drummers begin rehearsing. The young man arrives at the ceremony having left behind the things of his youth so he can embark on the sacred passage to adulthood.

Because the teen years are often difficult for youngsters, considerable care is needed at home as well. Try not to be put off by your teen's new choices in clothing, hairstyle, friends, and modes of self-expression. Remember what it was like when you were a teenager—how you wanted to follow certain trends and be around people your parents disapproved of. Regardless of how "altered" your teen may look, it's important to show your love and be available to help out with problems. Plan family meals where everyone converses together, and hold family meetings to give your child more opportunities for family input. Know who your teen spends time with. Be open, caring, and understanding.

This is a crucial time to teach respect for Mother Earth as well, by practicing it yourself and also guiding your youngster. Cherokee youth learn such lessons through everyday experiences. If a teen breaks a limb off a tree, he is told that the tree is hurting just as he would be if someone tugged at his arm or leg. If he throws a stone at someone, he is informed that this mistreatment has upset the stone's spirit. The teen is then advised to apologize to the spirit of the tree or stone and say that he would like to be forgiven for the harm he has caused. Such practices help youngsters realize that everything in nature is alive and deserves respect. If you insist on respect for human life and Mother Earth, and if you live what you teach, your teenager will carry these teachings.

Raising Children to Heal Society

Over the past couple of centuries, people caused so much pain to one another and to Mother Earth that humankind is now paying steep dues, in the form of rampant destruction and death. Because children brought into today's world are facing the cumulative injuries caused by their ancestors, they require special attentiveness from mothers and fathers willing to parent with a purpose—the healing of society.

We live in an angry society where many parents don't love their teenagers, or anyone else's. Most teens, in turn, have lost respect for their parents, themselves, and everything around them. This is the legacy that has been left to us, and with it comes a great need for correction. To begin, teach your child good values from the start, for then she will demonstrate them to others. Speak to your child about love, hug her often, and show how deeply you care about her, for then she will grow up with a caring heart. And day by day clear yourself of hurts so you can continue to express your love and caring, because that is the healing medicine. (For help with personal clearing, see "An Inventory for Balanced Parenting" on pages 109–114.)

Continue these practices throughout the teen years, as your child steps more fully into society. In particular, build upon the groundwork you have established for healthy communication. For example, give your teenager a cell phone or calling card so she can contact you while away from home. Also maintain an attitude of openness and trust. Nothing should be "off limits" for parent and teen discussions.

Love, caring, and communication—all means for healing society—come into dynamic play at family meetings. So every two to four weeks hold a meeting in which each member speaks the truth about any problems and positive results they are experiencing. To ensure that everyone has a chance to speak, you could use a "talking stick" approach, a method of communication that has been very successful in Cherokee culture. The person speaking holds the stick until they have finished talking then passes it to the next person. After everyone has spoken, it is time to discuss solutions to the problems that were shared, agreeing on the best ways to deal with them. Should anyone become angry, they are given a chance to speak, after which the focus returns to the issues at hand. In addition, family members celebrate the good events that were described. Meetings end with everyone hugging and declaring their love for one another.

Raising children to heal society also means teaching them how nature nurtures their body and spirit, and instilling respect for all living things. Talk to your child about trees, plants, animals, birds, even insects, and about roles they play in preserving the fabric of life on earth. Emphasize respect for the environment, revealing in an age-appropriate manner the consequences of destroying trees, killing animals, polluting streams and rivers, and other actions that disrupt the balance of nature. In the teen years, especially, point out how everything we need for a strong and healthy life comes from the natural world. Your teenager may then be among those who stand up and champion Mother Earth.

Meditation

- Sit comfortably in a chair with your back straight, and quiet your thoughts.

- Take a deep breath, pulling it gently into your stomach, then let the breath out slowly.

- As you continue breathing slowly and deeply, concentrate on your concerns about child rearing.

- When you feel relaxed, ask the Creator for whatever help you need for yourself or your child. Keep breathing slowly, allowing all emotions to surface.

- When you are ready to end the meditation, slowly count to 12 and open your eyes.

- Journal what you have received from the meditation.

PART III

Children As Future Caretakers of Mother Earth

Teaching Care
for Mother Earth

Mother Earth is the foundation of life. Without her we would not be here. All people know this, but all people do not respect it. Since children are the next generation of caretakers of Mother Earth, we must teach them this respect from an early age.

Traditionally, Native Americans are taught how to respect Mother Earth. I clearly remember being told by elders, "If you respect her, she will take care of you. If you give her pain, she will store it and the turtle will later shake its back." The turtle represents North America, and this teaching means that if North Americans do not nurture Mother Earth she will respond with disruptions here, such as storms, earthquakes, or flooding. Our relationship to Mother Earth should therefore be one of loving reciprocity: we nurture her and she will care for us. When we teach care for Mother Earth, we ensure the strength needed to help our children gain inner freedom.

Cherokee children are taught to respect Mother Earth in a way that does not hamper their natural development. We recognize that if you repeatedly say "no" to children when they're about to do something disrespectful of Mother Earth, they will soon ignore the command. So instead, we tell them why something shouldn't be done. Once children understand the consequences of their actions, they not only refrain from such behavior but also remind others to do so. Children who notice a youngster doing harm to the earth will usually tell him to stop, and if that doesn't work they'll ask an elder to speak to him.

Another teaching tool in Cherokee culture is the custom of having children set a place for Mother Earth at the family table. This becomes a tangible reminder of her role in their lives. Children raised with these traditions continue to honor Mother Earth as adults and pass the teachings on to the next generation.

Attaining Balance of Nature and Life

*L*ife is given by the Creator not to be destroyed but to be maintained in balance with all of nature. Unfortunately, through arrogance or ignorance people have made even the basic elements of life—air and water—unclean, threatening this healthy balance. As a child I predicted, "In the future, we will be wearing oxygen masks and paying for air, and we will drink our water from bottles." I could see these unnatural practices on the horizon, but I had no idea that at least one would materialize within decades. Nor did I grasp the cost of such practices in terms of physical, mental, emotional, and spiritual illnesses.

It is time to once again live in balance with Mother Earth and resume the caretaking role given to us by the Creator, for only then will Mother Earth be able to provide healthy, natural lives for our children. Common sense reveals many things an individual can do, such as picking up trash and refusing to contribute to chemical waste-dumps. Cherokee people additionally advocate for a halt to the large-scale acceleration of environmental stagnation through the slaughtering of animals and the clear-cutting of trees. To clean Mother Earth is to cleanse ourselves, for we feel every pain she registers in response to our mistreatment of her. Imagine Mother Earth feeling so cared for that she wraps her arms around you and gives you and your child clean air, pure water, and good health.

Living in balance with all of nature requires us also to live in harmony with one another. Harmony comes not from subscribing to a particular belief system but from honoring the traditions of all cultures and the rights of all people, provided that they do not violate our own. Cooperation between cultures goes a long way toward fulfilling the sacred purpose of life.

Restoring
Land and Cultures

*T*he treatment of indigenous cultures is the same today as it was when invaders came to this land, only instead of cannons and swords the warring people have automatic machine guns and high-tech weapons that destroy entire generations. Some nations are now gone forever.

Wherever they go, the warring ones take life. They ravage the rain forest, which provides stability of plant life. Then they annihilate its native people and their distinctive way of life given by the Creator.

What has happened? Why are people who were once so free in the world of nature no longer permitted to have land and walk with dignity on Mother Earth? How could others searching for freedom have been so inhumane to them? It is because the warring ones came with orders from their leaders rather than with the good teachings of the Creator. And because they killed people and raped the land, taking what did not belong to them, they further distanced themselves from the Creator. As a result, the fighting, killing, pain, and sadness continue. Despite all hopes for the new millennium, we still have not gotten in touch with our true selves well enough to discover that we can't control everything and that there is a higher force than technology.

This job now falls to our children as future caretakers of Mother Earth. It will be up to them to reveal that technology unaccompanied by respect spawns the mistaken notion that humans have the capacity to control the Creator's realms. For our part, we can encourage our children to think about Mother Earth and her many gifts. We can invite their discoveries of truth. In teaching our children, we—and they—have a chance to help form a caring society. At the same time, we can pray to the Creator to restore the land and diverse cultures for the health of humanity.

Solidarity for Survival

*A*lone, parents can do only so much. But by coming together with shared vision and harmonious ways, we could collaborate in fostering a generation of true environmental stewards, for there is great strength in numbers.

To establish common ground at the outset, we might agree on four basic child-rearing tenets. First, it is important that the mother nurture the child as much as possible from the time of birth, so they bond. The father bond, developed through holding and spending undistracted time with the child, is likewise nurturing. Children who have close bonds with their parents form close bonds with the earth.

Second, the child needs a cultural identity rooted in the parents' values. In Cherokee culture, this identity is traditionally cultivated by the grandparents; in their absence it is shaped by the parents. Children who grow up relating deeply to their cultural heritage experience a powerful relationship to their earthly home.

Third, the child benefits from parental agreement about rules and routines. This consensus prevents the child from feeling confused or torn by domestic disputes. Having grown up in such a setting, she will know how to keep her words and actions aligned and how to find mutuality with others. Children raised in an atmosphere of balance and harmony later bring these forces to their interactions with the earth.

Fourth, as the child gains independence it is essential to remain aware of her well-being and intervene with corrective guidance should she come in contact with harmful influences. Children accustomed to parental vigilance take on the mantle of planetary vigilance, remaining watchful and equipped to counteract destructive forces.

Together, we can prepare our children to be caretakers of the earth. Just as Native people, despite a diversity of traditions, share an understanding about the purpose of life and the need to care for Mother Earth, so can parents of all backgrounds share this understanding. To bring your vision of tomorrow's children to fruition, you may need to reevaluate your thinking and clear your mind and heart of the anger and pain you have experienced in life. Once you do that, you can look to the future and join with other parents in raising the next generation to care for Mother Earth and, in return, receive her care.

Vision for the Future of Children

Our vision as parents is one and the same. We want to see our children stand tall, reflecting the values with which they were raised and proud of who they are. We want to hear them speak with conviction about their cultural traditions and offer thanks for everything given to them by the Creator. We want our children to feel the happiness and freedom that is their birthright.

There will come a time when mothers will cry with joy knowing that their children are free to live with dignity on this land. Hunger will be gone, and their children will feel no pain. The Creator, embracing them all, will then teach them what has been forgotten for generations.

Preparing for Future Generations

According to Cherokee teachings, we are to prepare the way for the seventh generation to come. This means ensuring optimum conditions on Mother Earth so that the seventh generation from today's may flourish. Our mission involves educating people in preventing habitat destruction and depletion of natural resources. It also calls for restoring balance to the environment and cleaning up Mother Earth so all seventh-generation inhabitants will have fresh water, healthy air, and trees to keep it pure. In connection with this, we express ongoing gratitude to the Creator for all that has been put here to help us live, such as the soil that lets us grow food nourishing to our bodies, the water that sustains the growth of plants, and the animals that transport sacred messages. The Cherokee people want each successive generation to carry on these teachings of the elders, giving Mother Earth and her people a better chance for a healthier life.

Much can be done on a daily basis to restore balance to Mother Earth for future generations. We can teach ourselves and our children about the soil and the beings who live on and within the earth; about water and its many beings; about the animals and the spirits they carry; about the rain, the sun, and the moon. We can pick up litter and join environmental groups working for the earth's well-being, such as discouraging the use of chemicals on crops that impact animal and human life. Our children, following our example, will then teach their children, gifting Mother Earth with cycles of restoration.

We must stand strong and be good teachers. If we look for ways to keep Mother Earth balanced, so will our children. Then one day all people will be able to enjoy a healthy life and a stronger connection to the Creator.

Meditation

- Sit or lie comfortably on Mother Earth, or lean against a tree.

- Closing your eyes, breathe slowly and deeply.

- Continue breathing slowly until your mind is calm and you are totally relaxed.

- Focus on the healing of the earth, imagining the soil ridding itself of chemicals and pollution coming to an end.

- Meditate on this healing for as long as possible. Then come out of the meditation by counting to 10.

- Journal your memories of the meditation.

An Inventory for Balanced Parenting

A personal inventory, if taken before becoming a parent and again throughout each stage of parenthood, reveals areas where further development may be needed to achieve inner balance as a mother or father. The inventory below contains twenty questions. Look within to find answers to them; return to the questions calling for deeper contemplation; then do whatever inner work is necessary to bring about the changes you desire. The more balanced you are as a parent, the easier it will be to provide your child with long-lasting sustenance.

1. **Who are you?**

   Knowing who you are has a great deal to do with knowing where your ancestors came from. The Creator gave everyone an original homeland. What's yours?

2. **What is the history of your people?**

   Acknowledge both the positive and negative aspects of your ancestors' history since together they help shape your identity.

3. Do you know what spirit is?

Spirit is the life force permeating everything on this earth and beyond. An understanding of spirit feeds your inner development, furnishes strength for your life's journey, and connects you to all other forms of energy in the universe.

4. Are you of good spirit?

Reviewing your accomplishments, see if you respect them. Practicing this respect in everyday life, and encouraging others to do the same, is to be of good spirit.

5. Do you use alcohol, drugs, or other substances that hurt your body and disrupt your mind?

If so, get help to free yourself from these harmful influences.

6. Do you need emotional support or guidance?

If you do, find people who can assist you in a spirit-based way.

7. Are you a victim of abuse?

   If so, seek counseling, as well as information about the effects of abuse. Physical, sexual, emotional, and mental cruelty all come from people who are out of control and using others to gain personal power.

8. Do you take care of yourself?

   If not, learn to nurture yourself so you can better nurture your child.

9. Do you associate with the elderly?

   Relationships with the elderly can deepen your respect for all of life. Learn to see these people as your teachers.

10. What don't you like about yourself?

    The traits and characteristics you don't like are affecting your self-image. Find ways to improve these tendencies by altering your routines and attitudes, getting counseling if necessary, and asking the Creator for hope. Or simply work on letting them go.

11. What do you like about yourself?

    The traits and characteristics you like inspire you to feel good about yourself. Bring them to expression often.

12. How can you improve yourself?

    Do you want to feel more motivated, more hopeful, freer, or better directed? Make a list of self-improvement goals and do your best to accomplish them.

13. Is your health as good as possible?

    Assess your physical health by getting a check-up. Then learn better ways to take care of yourself and improve your overall well-being.

14. Have you thought about death?

    Consider that death is not bad or terminal. In Cherokee culture, we are taught that death is a long journey taken to the Spirit World in the Creator's land, where the person's spirit continues to grow.

15. If you already have a child, how involved are you in parenting?

If your child is an infant, does he receive round-the-clock parental care in the home? If your child is older, do you listen to him and offer guidance? If your child is a teenager, do you encourage open communication and pay close attention to his concerns? If you are not giving your child sufficient care and guidance, seek out more information, a support group, or counseling.

16. Are you working to heal your inner self?

The first step in healing the inner self is to recognize any pain, anger, sadness, or loneliness that may be blocking access to your spirit and obstructing your vision of the future. The next step is to clear your mind and heart of the distress, either on your own or with professional help from someone you trust.

17. Do you feel negative toward other people because of their race, skin color, or religion?

If you do, get in touch with your feelings and motivations, then work toward increased awareness and tolerance.

18. Do you feel victimized by personal circumstances?

If feelings of victimization are causing you to see your-self as weak and powerless, recognize that you have lost contact with the potent energies of your inner spirit. To reestablish this contact, free yourself of inner burdens by connecting with the forces of nature, or seek spiritual guidance from a trusted friend or counselor.

19. Are you grounded or ungrounded?

To be grounded is to be true to your beliefs and ca-pable of reaching your goals. To be ungrounded is to lack strong convictions and means for accomplishing your goals. If you are ungrounded, check in with your-self every morning upon waking and modify any unrealistic goals you have set for the day.

20. Do you thank the Creator for all that has been given to you?

Expressions of gratitude for good fortune keep open your channel of communication with the Creator. If you are going through hard times, still give thanks to the Creator, for difficulties usher in valuable lessons.

Meditation

- Sit or lie in a comfortable place. Breathe in deeply, then slowly breathe out. Repeat this process 5 to 8 times.

- Visualize yourself walking through a sunny green valley resplendent with trees and wildflowers, and overhead a bright blue sky with white clouds. Picture a lake and go for a swim, or just sit by the water enjoying the surroundings.

- Continuing your walk up a hill, sit comfortably at the top and take in the panoramic view.

- Now imagine yourself falling asleep and dreaming the material you have read in this book. Upon waking, picture yourself feeling invigorated. Notice someone handing you a beautiful flower and sitting with you in silence before leaving.

❖ Then walk down the hill to the lake and conclude the mediation by counting very slowly to 10.

❖ Remain in position for a while, then journal what you have experienced.

❖ Consider the kind of flower you were given and the person who gave it to you. Reflect on what this might mean for your life. Be aware of how receiving the gift of a flower in this landscape connects you to Mother Earth and to spirit.

❖ Return to this awareness as you guide your child into each new day.

About the Author

Tsolagiu M.A. RuizRazo lives with her husband Rahkweeskeh and their three wolves and two dogs on thirty-seven acres of wooded land in the mountains of New Tazewell, Tennessee. A Cherokee Wolf Clan elder, Tsolagiu is widely respected for her spiritual gifts, which she uses to bridge the Spirit World and everyday existence for people close to home and around the world. She is the mother of two grown children and grandmother of a two year old. She also travels throughout the United States, Canada, Mexico, and Europe teaching indigenous wisdom.

When she is not traveling, Tsolagiu operates a home business, TMAR Human Development and Stress Release, Inc., where she and her husband offer counseling services in workplace and personal relations. In addition, she is the founder and director of Traditional Native Survival Cultural Center, Inc., a nonprofit organization that educates Native people in their culture and spirituality.

Dedicated to preserving the environment for future generations, she advocates for reconnecting the inner self with the natural world. Tsolagiu's first book, *Spirit of the White Wolf Woman*, is a collection of poems to assist in overcoming the hardships of daily life.

ORDER FORM

Quantity	Amount
_____ *Tomorrow's Children: A Cherokee Elder's Guide to Parenting* ($14.95)	_____
_____ *Spirit of the White Wolf Woman* ($19.95)	_____
Sales tax of 9.25% for Tennessee residents	_____
Shipping & handling ($3.00 for first book; $1.00 for each additional book)	_____
Total amount enclosed	_____

Quantity discounts available

Method of payment

❏ Check or money order enclosed (made payable to **World Edition, USA** in US currency only)

❏ MasterCard ❏ VISA _____

_____   _____
signature   expiration date

Please photocopy this order form, fill it out, and mail it, together with your personal check, money order, or charge-card information, to:

World Edition, USA
PO Box 1284
New Tazewell, TN 37824
423-626-5450